THE GOLFER'S
EXCUSE HANDBOOK

Golfertainment for Good and Bad Golfers

KURT TAYLOR

CONTENTS

Chapter 5:
Whether Or Not The
Weather Can Weather It .. 79

Chapter 4:
A Spectator Sport 60

Conclusion 97

INTRODUCTION

Anyone who has ever tried to swing a golf club has undoubtedly experienced the dread of a bad golf shot. For those, who have experienced many of those bad golf shots, have likely learned that a good joke can help to ease the tension for themselves, and also ease the discomfort of the poor people unlucky enough to witness it. And since golf is a game that has been around for hundreds of years, millions of golfers have had to come up with their own jokes.

With that history in mind, this book seeks to bring you some of the funniest, or most outrageous, shot excuses ever made on the golf course. Maybe you'll remember some of your favorites to recite the next time your ball finds a landing spot that isn't the short grass or the bottom of the cup.

This book is separated into chapters, and each chapter will be dedicated to exactly who's at fault for the bad shot. So, whether it's the equipment, the user, the witnesses, or the course itself, there will be excuses galore.

If you've received this book as a gift, don't consider it a sign that you hit enough bad golf shots to need the information in these pages. Instead, be excited for the opportunity to hit your playing partners with a new one-liner that catches them off guard. You never know, it might just give you the advantage you need in your next match, or at least keep others from feeling bad for you and all of the balls lost during the round.

Regardless of your situation, the ultimate goal is to bring a smile to you, the reader. The game of golf is beautiful and frustrating beyond measure, so everyone should bond over their shared frustrations. Let's not waste any more time, then. Time to tee up the excuses!

CHAPTER 1:

ALL ON ME

In this chapter, you'll find a fine collection of excuses that focus on you, the one who committed that inevitable act of a poor, likely laughable golf shot. So, one great way to deflect any rising anger or disappointment is to give in. Be part of the laughs and move on. These lines will help you on your path to redemption! Well, they'll at least make you smile.

I get one mulligan per hole,
that's my handicap.

GOLF SCORECARD

HOLE	1	2	3	4	5	6	7	8	9	OUT	IN	TOT
BLUE	356	527	194	379	427	313	615	436	204	3511	3461	6502
GREEN	332	513	163	344	406	357	543	432	174	3243	3222	6465
GREY	314	506	136	296	329	341	498	369	137	2926	2865	5791
HANDICAP	13	3	15	11	7	9	5	1	17			
ME	7											
MULLIGANS	-1											
ME AFTER	6											
MULLIGANS												
PAR	4	5	5	4	4	4	5	4	4	36	36	72
GREEN	311	413	118	282	326	289	488	295	295	2656	2850	5352
LADIE'S	13	3	15	11	9	5	1	7	7			
DATE:				SCORER:				ATTEST:				

EXCUSES

• 1 •

I wasted the good shot on a practice swing.

• 2 •

I thought I was using a different club.

• 3 •

I get one mulligan per hole, that's my handicap.

• 4 •

I just haven't played this course before.

• 5 •

I was overconfident after my last round.

EXCUSES

• 6 •

This is my first round of the year,
so I'm getting back into the rhythm.

• 7 •

Well, I should have laid up instead of going for it.

• 8 •

That's the last time I try to hold
the putter cross-handed.

• 9 •

A bead of sweat dropped into my eye
just as I was making contact.

• 10 •

Boy, I hit it off the toe of the club on that one.

EXCUSES

• 11 •

I just couldn't get my footing comfortable.

• 12 •

I think I pulled a muscle in my back on the last hole.

• 13 •

I need to play early rounds more often;
I'm still waking up.

• 14 •

I'm so excited to see where it goes that
I'm lifting my head way too early.

• 15 •

I've been lifting more weights lately,
so all of my club distances are changing.

GOLF QUOTES

1

Golf is a game whose aim is to get a very small ball into an even smaller hole with weapons singularly ill-designed for the purpose.

– Winston Churchill

2

They call it golf because all the other four-letter words were taken.

– Ray Floyd

3

The most important shot in golf is the next one.

– Ben Hogan

I've been lifting more weights lately,
so all of my club distances are changing.

EXCUSES

• 16 •

I should have trusted my first
thought on that one.

• 17 •

Business has been going well,
but it's cutting into my practice time.

• 18 •

I didn't have the chance to practice this
course on my VR headset beforehand.

• 19 •

It's hard to concentrate right now.
My ex's funeral starts in about 10 minutes.

• 20 •

I stubbed my toe yesterday,
so the balance in my stance is a little off.

EXCUSES

• 21 •

I don't know what I expected when
I only play once a year.

• 22 •

I usually need a burger at the turn.
I think I'm feeling a little weak without it.

• 23 •

My sunscreen is running into my eyes.

• 24 •

I'll be able to shoot my age in about 60 years.

• 25 •

I think keeping my head down makes
me get under the ball too much.

DID YOU KNOW?

• 1 •

The golf ball was first made from leather
pouches filled with cows' hair.

• 2 •

Modern golf was invented in Scotland
around 1457, and then was promptly
banned in the country for almost 300 years.

• 3 •

Your chances, as an average golfer, of making
a hole-in-one are 12,500 to one.

• 4 •

The average golfer who walks during
their round will burn 430 calories per hour.

• 5 •

Today's golf ball has between 300
and 500 dimples on its surface.

I ate way too much at breakfast this morning and reaching around this gut is not an easy task.

EXCUSES

• 26 •

I must have looked at the scorecard upside down
because I thought this dogleg went the other way.

• 27 •

My putting is stronger from longer distances.

• 28 •

It's hard to mentally recover from
what happened on the front nine.

• 29 •

My footing was way too close to the ball.

• 30 •

My score would have been great
if it wasn't for that 12 that I carded.

EXCUSES

• 31 •

It feels like my shoulder injury from
high school is flaring up today.

• 32 •

Ever since I shot 75, I've been playing terribly.

• 33 •

I was in between clubs on that shot.

• 34 •

I played for a fade, but it came out as a draw.

• 35 •

I think I used up all of the
good ones on the range today.

GOLF QUOTES

1

They say golf is like life, but don't believe them.
Golf is more complicated than that.

– Gardner Dickinson

2

I would like to deny all allegations by Bob Hope
that during my last game of golf, I hit an eagle,
a birdie, an elk, and a moose.

– Gerald Ford

3

Always throw your clubs ahead of you.
That way, you don't have to waste energy
going back to pick them up.

– Tommy Bolt

EXCUSES

• 36 •

I think the bad round I had yesterday
is still affecting my confidence.

• 37 •

I ate way too much at breakfast this morning,
and reaching around this gut is not an easy task.

• 38 •

I'm used to playing from the tops,
not the amateur tees.

• 39 •

My swing is too much like my hockey shot.

• 40 •

I lost a contact lens, and now
I can't see any landing areas.

I went after it too hard and took too much grass.

EXCUSES

• 41 •

My last surgery is really affecting my play.

• 42 •

I only get to play once every six months.

• 43 •

I gave up on my follow-through for that shot.

• 44 •

I went after it too hard and took too much grass.

• 45 •

I over-rotated my hips on that one.

DID YOU KNOW?

• 1 •

Of all registered golfers,
80% have a handicap higher than 18.

• 2 •

The only nudist golf course
in the world is located in France.

• 3 •

Players used small mounds of sand
before tees were invented.

• 4 •

The first image of golf is from a 1740's
painting of St. Andrews Golf Links.

• 5 •

An ace on a par 5 is called a condor.

EXCUSES

• 46 •

That was actually my practice swing,
but I made contact on accident.

• 47 •

I laid up because I thought this was a par 5.

• 48 •

I always forget to let my wrists break on contact.

• 49 •

I had to skip my round last week
because I was too hungover.

• 50 •

I was getting 20 extra yards on the
driving range this morning.

EXCUSES

• 51 •

My ingrown toenail is messing with my stance.

• 52 •

My swing speed is finally catching up to my age.

• 53 •

I need those sweet spot markers for my
clubs because I can't find solid contact.

• 54 •

I play my best golf when there's money on the line.

• 55 •

I never play on Sundays because
there's no morning beer.

CHAPTER 2:
MIXED BAG

This set of excuses turns the focus away from the user and onto that blasted equipment in your bag. Whether or not your friends will believe you is another problem altogether.

But really, we all know it wasn't you.

This new bag is way too heavy;
I'm getting tired just walking to my ball.

EXCUSES

• 56 •

This driver is brand new,
so I'm still getting used to it.

• 57 •

These tees are keeping the ball too high.

• 58 •

The grip on my putter is falling apart.
I can't hold it properly.

• 59 •

I left my lucky ball marker at home.

• 60 •

My wedding ring is too big under my glove.

EXCUSES

• 61 •

This new bag is way too heavy;
I'm getting tired just walking to my ball.

• 62 •

My shoelace will not stay tied.

• 63 •

I think this putter is off-balance.

• 64 •

These clubs are too long,
but I choked down too far and topped the ball.

• 65 •

These plastic spikes are not doing me any favors.

GOLF QUOTES

1

I have a tip that can take five strokes off
anyone's game. It's called an eraser.

– Arnold Palmer

2

Golf is a day spent in a round
of strenuous idleness.

– William Wordsworth

3

Hockey is a sport for white men. Basketball is
a sport for black men. Golf is a sport for white
men dressed like black pimps.

– Tiger Woods

EXCUSES

• 66 •

I'm used to carrying an extra
fairway wood in my bag.

• 67 •

My ball was scuffed by the cart path,
so it didn't roll well on the green.

• 68 •

These sunglasses have a different
tint than the ones I'm used to.

• 69 •

I accidentally put my glove in the dryer,
and now it doesn't fit.

• 70 •

That iron definitely needs to be regripped
because it's slipping in my hands.

The shaft on this driver has too much flex in it.

EXCUSES

· 71 ·

My wife ordered me the wrong glove size.

· 72 ·

I had to throw away my lucky shirt; it ran out of luck.

· 73 ·

These red golf balls are hard for me
to track through the air.

· 74 ·

These shoes must have warped
because my feet are killing me.

· 75 ·

I've never been able to get that
distance out of this club before.

DID YOU KNOW?

• 1 •

Hot weather allows golf balls to travel farther.

• 2 •

Annika Sorenstam was the first female golfer
to shoot a round of 59 in competitive play.

• 3 •

The first dogleg was invented by Scottish
golfer Tom Morris in the 19th century.

• 4 •

Golf was the first sport (out of two)
to ever be played on the moon.

• 5 •

Sam Snead and Tiger Woods are tied
with the most PGA wins at 82.

EXCUSES

· 76 ·

The shaft on this driver has too much flex in it.

· 77 ·

I left the club I wanted to use at home.

· 78 ·

This shirt is clinging to me,
and it's messing up my swing.

· 79 ·

I think these tees are interfering with my contact.

· 80 ·

Is my ball flying oddly?
I think it might be damaged.

EXCUSES

· 81 ·

The grooves in the face of my wedge are worn down,
so I can't get any spin going.

· 82 ·

I think my chance of losing a ball is higher
when I'm using a brand new ball.

· 83 ·

I think my cat has been scratching at the club grips.

· 84 ·

I have a hard time keeping the club
face open with that wedge.

· 85 ·

Amazing contact, just used the wrong club.

I think my cat has been scratching at the club grips.

GOLF QUOTES

1

Golf is the closest game to the game we call life.
You get bad breaks from good shots;
you get good breaks from bad shots—but you
have to play the ball where it lies.

– Bobby Jones

2

Swing hard in case you hit it.

– Dan Marino

3

We learn so many things from
golf—how to suffer, for instance.

– Bruce Lansky

EXCUSES

• 86 •

This wedge doesn't get as much loft as my old one.

• 87 •

They don't make my favorite golf shoes anymore.

• 88 •

These irons are too short for me.

• 89 •

I'm afraid my golf bag might
be home to a family of spiders.

• 90 •

I'm experimenting with a new ball today,
and I can't judge the spin on it yet.

EXCUSES

• 91 •

I think my wedge's shaft has a tiny dent in it.

• 92 •

This new driver has less loft,
so my ball doesn't take the path I want it to take.

• 93 •

Actually, this entire set of clubs is getting old;
I should replace them soon.

• 94 •

I lost a spike in my shoe.

• 95 •

I went for more backspin,
but the ball wouldn't cooperate.

DID YOU KNOW?

• 1 •

The first international golf competition took place in 1682 between Scotland and England.

• 2 •

Gene Sarazen invented the modern sand wedge and debuted it in 1932, where he won 'The Open Championship'.

• 3 •

Women's golf began in 1811.

• 4 •

A rule granting free relief for an embedded ball first emerged in 1773.

• 5 •

The first 18-hole course in the United States was the Chicago Golf Club, built in 1893.

I'm afraid my golf bag might
be home to a family of spiders.

EXCUSES

• 96 •

I broke my good putter last week.

• 97 •

The golf pants I'm wearing are too tight,
and I can't rotate my hips around.

• 98 •

My stroke counter malfunctioned.
Just give me a par.

• 99 •

The glove I usually use in the rain
must still be at home.

• 100 •

This sand wedge is not heavy enough
to cut through the sand.

EXCUSES

• 101 •

I forgot to wash my golf towel, and now it's useless.

• 102 •

This putter does not want to stay square to the ball.

• 103 •

I don't have the same power with these new irons.

• 104 •

These novelty tees break too easily.

• 105 •

This knee brace isn't meant for golf play.

CHAPTER 3:

WHERE THE GREEN GRASS GROWS

Well, sometimes the grass is green. Other times, it might be brown. And, on the worst of times, there's a nice hard-packed patch of earth right in the middle of the fairway. What could be a better target for your excuse? Let's take a look at some of the best ones that focus on the course itself.

The course layout is confusing.
I thought THAT was the green we were aiming for.

EXCUSES

• 106 •

These pin placements are ridiculous.
The grounds' crew must be mad at someone today.

• 107 •

The course layout is confusing.
I thought THAT was the green we were aiming for.

• 108 •

Why is this area considered out of bounds?
I can play it.

• 109 •

This green is a lot faster than the last one.

• 110 •

This course has way too many hills.

EXCUSES

• 111 •

There must be a different kind
of sand in these bunkers.

• 112 •

I can't believe they haven't trimmed that tree;
that low branch messed up my backswing.

• 113 •

The break on the green was impossible to read.

• 114 •

There's too much debris on the approach,
I can't find my ball.

• 115 •

I thought the dew would dry up faster than this.

GOLF QUOTES

1

Golf is my passion, so is a great barbeque.

– John Daly

2

Golf appeals to the idiot in us and the child. Just how childlike golfers become is proven by their frequent inability to count past five.

– John Updike

3

The game of golf would lose a great deal if croquet mallets and billiard cues were allowed on the putting green.

– Ernest Hemingway

EXCUSES

• 116 •

The pins keep tempting me to take riskier shots.

• 117 •

The tee area is all chewed up,
so I can't tee it up properly.

• 118 •

No chipping green on this course,
and now I've got the yips.

• 119 •

The yardage marker needs to be updated
here because there's no way I hit it short.

• 120 •

I'm used to playing on courses that are
much higher quality than this one.

The pins keep tempting me to take riskier shots.

EXCUSES

• 121 •

This bunker is hidden from the tee,
not sure that's fair.

• 122 •

I can't believe the bathroom is closed.
It's gonna be hard to concentrate.

• 123 •

The greens really needed a double-cut today.

• 124 •

The rough is way too thick out here
because it just stopped my ball.

• 125 •

My lie was bad because the cuts are too severe.

DID YOU KNOW?

• 1 •

Wooden golf clubs were originally made with ash,
hazel, and beech wood.

• 2 •

The first U.S. Open took place in 1895.

• 3 •

The world record for the most holes of
golf played in a single year is 14,625.

• 4 •

Every standard golf hole is 4.5 inches
wide and has been since 1891.

• 5 •

The first set of rules ever recorded was written in 1744
by the Honorable Company of Edinburgh Golfers.

EXCUSES

• 126 •

The putting green rolled a lot differently
than the greens out here.

• 127 •

The cart path shouldn't be so close to the green;
my ball hit it and went out of bounds.

• 128 •

The bunkers on this course must not get raked often,
because the sand is packed down.

• 129 •

That pond was smaller the last time I played here.

• 130 •

If there were pine trees instead of oaks,
I wouldn't lose my ball in the leaves.

EXCUSES

• 131 •

Since when did a red stake mean Out of Bounds?

• 132 •

Was the fairway really designed to be this narrow?

• 133 •

My last shot landed in a divot,
so it came out weird on contact.

• 134 •

That fairway bunker looks a lot smaller from the tee.

• 135 •

There's way too much sand on this green,
and it's sticking to my ball.

Was the fairway really designed to be this narrow?

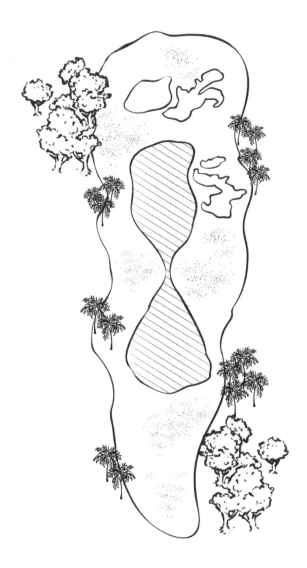

GOLF QUOTES

1

Reverse every natural instinct and do the
opposite of what you are inclined to do,
and you will probably come very close
to having a perfect golf swing.

– Ben Hogan

2

Golf is a good walk spoiled.

– Mark Twain

3

Golf is a fascinating game. I've taken nearly
40 years to discover that I can't play it.

– Ted Ray

EXCUSES

• 136 •

The range didn't have any balls available
this morning for my practice routine.

• 137 •

The course designer should not have
put such a severe slope on that green.

• 138 •

This bush was not here the last time I played,
so I should get relief.

• 139 •

I can't believe there's a low plug right in my line.

• 140 •

If the pin was in the front, like it should have been,
I'd have a tap-in for birdie!

EXCUSES

• 141 •

I wouldn't have played here if I knew
it was a walking course.

• 142 •

I just got an unlucky bounce off that slope;
I wonder if it was mowed properly.

• 143 •

That ball washer left some kind of film on my ball,
and now it's not flying right.

• 144 •

The scorecard says this pin was supposed
to be in a different spot.

• 145 •

These greens need to be cut shorter
because they are slow.

DID YOU KNOW?

• 1 •

Scotland's King James IV was the first
golfing ruler in the world (around 1500).

• 2 •

The last player to win a Major championship
with a wooden driver head is Bernhard Langer, in 1993.

• 3 •

The WPGA was founded in 1944, but folded in 1949.
The LPGA was created the next year, in 1950.

• 4 •

Golf balls are not permitted to weigh more than 1.62
ounces.

• 5 •

Arnold Palmer was the first golfer to win four
Masters tournaments in his career.

I lost my ball in that sinkhole over there.

EXCUSES

• 146 •

The cup was damaged, and it made my ball lip out.

• 147 •

The ball can't run down the fairways
when they're practically mud.

• 148 •

The Out-of-Bounds stakes should look
different from the 150 markers.

• 149 •

These carts don't have any speakers,
and I need music to help my rhythm.

• 150 •

Bermuda grass isn't a good fit for this climate.
Rye would be better.

EXCUSES

• 151 •

These fairways need more water because
there's barely any grass on them.

• 152 •

These tee markers are way too close together,
I can't get comfortable.

• 153 •

There should have been a yardage marker
around here, but it's gone.

• 154 •

I keep hitting my knee on the
dashboard of that golf cart.

• 155 •

I lost my ball in that sinkhole over there.

CHAPTER 4:
A SPECTATOR SPORT

Golf is a peaceful game that can be played alone. But, more often, there are others around you, and you know what? It's their fault that your shot was terrible! And, on top of that, you should let them know it's their fault with one of these lines.

Your ball marker is way too distracting,
just pick it up.

EXCUSES

• 156 •

Did you see all of those ball marks on the green?
Impossible to putt on that surface.

• 157 •

I heard someone sneeze during my backswing!

• 158 •

Nobody told me about the water hazard on this hole,
so I'd like a mulligan.

• 159 •

I just didn't want to hit into the group ahead of us.

• 160 •

Your ball marker is way too distracting,
just pick it up.

EXCUSES

• 161 •

Lots of planes flying around here;
that gets annoying pretty quickly.

• 162 •

I only play well when my playing partners play well.

• 163 •

That's the last time I listen to my swing coach.

• 164 •

Why is the grounds crew mowing
the rough so close to us?

• 165 •

How has the beer cart lady not been
around to see us yet? I need a beer.

GOLF QUOTES

1

I've heard people say putting is 50% technique
and 50% mental. I really believe it is 50%
technique and 90% positive thinking, see,
but that adds up to 140%, which is why
nobody is 100% sure how to putt.

– Chi Chi Rodriguez

2

Of all the hazards, fear is the worst.

– Sam Snead

3

Golf is not, and never has been, a fair game.

– Jack Nicklaus

EXCUSES

• 166 •

You are all playing badly and bringing
me down to your level.

• 167 •

My ex got my good set of clubs in the settlement.

• 168 •

Maybe if you all hadn't rushed me off the driving
range, I'd have gotten more practice swings in.

• 169 •

If you're going to keep smoking that
cigarette/pipe/cigar, could you stay off the tee box?

• 170 •

Your shadow kept me from reading
the break on the green.

Your shadow kept me from reading
the break on the green.

EXCUSES

· 171 ·

Your outfit is way too distracting.

· 172 ·

God must be mad that I came here
instead of going to church.

· 173 ·

My usual playing partners
would have given relief on that lie.

· 174 ·

The newborn at home won't let me get
any sleep, and now it's hurting my game.

· 175 ·

I wish that group behind us would
stop playing so quickly.

DID YOU KNOW?

• 1 •

The only golfer to complete a Grand Slam
(all four majors in one year) was Bobby Jones in 1930.

• 2 •

The Open Championship first took place in 1860.

• 3 •

Muirfield is a famous course in Scotland
created by Tom Morris in 1891.

• 4 •

Tiger Woods is the only modern golfer to hold all four
major championships at one time, although those
victories occurred over two years.

• 5 •

One of the most famous golf holes is the 17th hole
of the TPC Sawgrass in Florida, where an estimated
125,000 balls are lost to the water that almost
completely surrounds the green.

EXCUSES

· 176 ·

I told you to pull the pin once I rolled the ball;
it would have gone in!

· 177 ·

I think I'm going to speak to the grounds' crew
because the course played terribly.

· 178 ·

My coach told me to swing like that.
Might have to find a new one.

· 179 ·

You couldn't have given me a gimme on that putt?

· 180 ·

There are too many people out here and waiting
for so long between shots is throwing me off.

EXCUSES

• 181 •

There is no way your handicap is higher than mine.

• 182 •

Why are you able to play it so far
forward in your stance and I'm not?

• 183 •

I told my instructor that my short game
needed help, but he didn't listen.

• 184 •

I have to hit after all of you hit those great shots?

• 185 •

You're too competitive for me,
it's throwing me off and ruining the fun.

Is the ranger following us?
It's really distracting.

GOLF QUOTES

1

Many shots are spoiled at the last instant
by efforts to add a few more yards.

– Bobby Jones

2

I'm about five inches from being
an outstanding golfer. That's the distance
my left ear is from my right.

– Ben Crenshaw

3

I call upon all nations to do everything
they can to stop these terrorist killers.
Thank you. Now watch this drive.

– George W. Bush

EXCUSES

• 186 •

Maybe you can help me convince
my wife that I need more lessons.

• 187 •

I can't believe that the golf gods are out
to get me today; that was a perfect contact!

• 188 •

I hit it just like I was coached, but it still sliced.

• 189 •

Is the ranger following us? It's really distracting.

• 190 •

The group before us left a huge
ball mark that's right in my line.

EXCUSES

• 191 •

I only play poorly when I play with you.

• 192 •

Did you just walk across the tee in
the middle of my swing?

• 193 •

I get nervous when I know other
people are watching.

• 194 •

Someone didn't rake the bunker,
and my ball is in their footprint.

• 195 •

I don't think the grounds crew calibrated
the range finders in these carts.

DID YOU KNOW?

• 1 •

The Claret Jug was first awarded to the
Open Champion in 1872, but it was not ready for
presentation by the end of the tournament!

• 2 •

Golf came to America in 1659 but was banned because
the balls were damaging houses and hurting people.

• 3 •

Jack Nicklaus holds the record for the most
major championship victories with 18.

• 4 •

The largest margin of victory in a major golf
tournament belongs to Tiger Woods,
who won the 2000 U.S. Open by 15 shots.

• 5 •

The Ryder Cup, a team tournament between U.S.
and European players, first took place in 1927.

Your golf bag smells,
and it's throwing me off.

EXCUSES

• 196 •

You're taking way too long, and I can't play
well with so much time between shots.

• 197 •

If we had a fourth in the group, it would
give me more time to read the greens.

• 198 •

I think the beer cart lady ended her day
too soon because I need another beer.

• 199 •

Your golf bag smells, and it's throwing me off.

• 200 •

If I had left the pin in the cup,
I would have made the putt.

EXCUSES

• 201 •

You were flirting with the beer
cart lady during my swing!

• 202 •

I think the group ahead of us kicked
my ball into the rough.

• 203 •

Your advice on that putt was not very helpful.

• 204 •

That guy mowing his yard right there
could have waited until I hit.

• 205 •

Is that slow group going to let us play through?
I'm tired of waiting.

CHAPTER 5:

WHETHER OR NOT THE WEATHER CAN WEATHER IT

The natural beauty of a golf course can be awe-inspiring.
But, sometimes, nature itself can rear its head and
destroy your golf shot. Is your party going to argue when
you say that the weather has affected your game?
Convince them of the truth with these excuses.

Is anyone else worried about those geese getting too close to us?

EXCUSES

• 206 •

There's a ton of pollen in the air right now;
I can barely breathe.

• 207 •

The wet morning air is affecting my club grip.

• 208 •

Why is the wind only blowing during my shots?

• 209 •

I think the cold air is making my joints stiffen up.

• 210 •

Is anyone else worried about those
geese getting too close to us?

EXCUSES

• 211 •

This light rain is starting to run into my shoes.

• 212 •

Is lightning 10 miles away
a good excuse for a mulligan?

• 213 •

The heat and rain are making the grass grow
too quickly, it's slowing down the greens.

• 214 •

I'm not used to playing so late;
it's getting too cold!

• 215 •

The breeze made the tree branch fall on my ball!

GOLF QUOTES

1

If you drink, don't drive, don't even putt.

– Dean Martin

2

Golf is a game in which we shout, 'Fore', shoot six and write down five.

– Paul Harvey

3

If you think it's hard to meet new people, try picking up the wrong golf ball.

– Jack Lemmon

EXCUSES

• 216 •

Yesterday's storm washed all of the
good sand out of the bunkers.

• 217 •

The wind has been shifting all day,
so I can't predict what it's going to do.

• 218 •

Did you hear those birds cawing during
my backswing? It threw off my rhythm!

• 219 •

Did you see that bug deflect my putt?

• 220 •

This constant wind is starting to hurt my ears.

I can't get my club under the ball
when the ground is practically frozen.

EXCUSES

• 221 •

I can't get my club under the ball when
the ground is practically frozen.

• 222 •

The trees along this fairway are killing the grass.

• 223 •

This heat is making my grips get all sweaty.

• 224 •

Lots of bird feces on this green;
must be that time of year.

• 225 •

This course is laid out east/west,
so the sun is blinding me on every other hole.

DID YOU KNOW?

• 1 •

The Open Championship was played in
Northern Ireland in 1951, marking the first time
it was not played in Scotland or England.

• 2 •

Patty Berg won the first U.S. Women's Open in 1946.

• 3 •

The Green Jacket, awarded to the winner
of the Masters, was first worn by members
of Augusta National from 1937-1948.

• 4 •

An unplayable lie was first defined
in golf rules back in 1759.

• 5 •

The Solheim Cup, a women's international team
tournament similar to the men's Ryder Cup,
was first established in 1990.

EXCUSES

• 226 •

The altitude here must be
affecting the wind speed.

• 227 •

This fog is making it really
hard to track my ball.

• 228 •

That tree is a lot wider than it looks.

• 229 •

My coach had to cancel my lesson this
week because of those storms.

• 230 •

I think a fly went into my ear just
as I was making contact.

EXCUSES

• 231 •

The wind brought my ball to a stop in midair.

• 232 •

The frost delayed our tee time,
and now I have to play faster.

• 233 •

The heat is drying out the greens,
and now they roll way too fast.

• 234 •

I think I hear a beehive over here,
so I'm going to take relief.

• 235 •

The sun keeps creating a glare off the lake.

I think I hear a beehive over here,
so I'm going to take relief.

GOLF QUOTES

1

The ball retriever is not long enough
to get my putter out of the tree.

– Brian Weiss

2

I was three over. One over a house,
one over a patio, and one over a swimming pool.

– George Brett

3

Like chess, golf is a game that is forever
challenging but can never be conquered.

– Harvey Penick

EXCUSES

• 236 •

All of that rain is creating hazards
on the fairway, it's unplayable.

• 237 •

This heat is making me drink too much water,
and now I'm bloated.

• 238 •

It must be mating season because
those ducks are really loud.

• 239 •

The rain this morning made the greens too slow.

• 240 •

How is the wind blowing into
my face on every hole?

EXCUSES

• 241 •

There must be something burning nearby,
there's a weird haze that's making my eyes water.

• 242 •

The hurricane made this course into
something completely different.

• 243 •

This cold air makes it hurt to swing the club.

• 244 •

I think the air pressure is making
the ball travel further.

• 245 •

The clouds are casting weird shadows on the green.

DID YOU KNOW?

• 1 •

Golf has only appeared at four summer Olympics:
1900, 1904, 2016, and 2020.

• 2 •

Although champions are supposed to leave
their Green Jackets at Augusta National,
Gary Player was the first golfer to take
his jacket out of the United States.

• 3 •

The idea that a ball must be played where
it lies was put into rulebooks in 1775.

• 4 •

The green was first distinguished as a
distinct feature of the golf course in 1812.

• 5 •

Tee markers were not invented until 1882!

The clouds are casting weird
shadows on the green.

EXCUSES

• 246 •

I think the sunlight is giving me a headache.

• 247 •

How is the wind affecting my ball on the green?

• 248 •

The hot air has me feeling too loose.

• 249 •

I want to move my ball out from under that dead tree
because I'm worried about it falling on me.

• 250 •

I'm rushing to finish before
the thunderstorm gets here.

CONCLUSION

So, there you have it. Two hundred and fifty excuses that have all been uttered at one time or another out there on the links. You likely found some that made you laugh, and probably more than a few that made your eyes roll in exasperation. Tell your golfing buddies that you're ready for their shenanigans, and maybe have a few more surprising lines of your own.

Remember, golf is a difficult game. There's no shame in spitting out an excuse every now and then to relieve some of that pressure. Make some good shots and make good memories out of the bad ones.

Made in United States
Orlando, FL
28 October 2023